THIS BOOK BELONGS TO:

NO PART OF THIS BOOK MAY BE REPRODUCED WITHOUT WRITTEN PERMISSION FROM THE AUTHOR

NO PART OF THIS BOOK MAY BE REPRODUCED WITHOUT WRITTEN PERMISSION FROM THE AUTHOR

no part of this book may be
reproduced without written
permission from the author

no part of this book may be
reproduced without written
permission from the author

Printed in Great Britain
by Amazon